How to Draw Koalas Step by Step (This How to Draw Koalas Book Shows How to Draw 39 Different Koalas Easily)

This book on how to draw koalas will be useful if you want to learn how to draw koala faces, koala pictures or anything to do with Koalas

James Manning

How to Draw Koalas

Introduction for Parents

Drawing is an essential part of a child's development, stimulating parts of the brain that are responsible for creative thinking and imagination. From a young age, we are all creatively encouraged to draw, whether it be at home or pre-school. Drawing is often encouraged to improve our fine motor skills and hand-eye co-ordination; this co-ordination is vital for future academic success and for improving our penmanship/handwriting skills.

From toddler's 'scribbles' to more refined 'matchstick men' and recognisable shapes, you may find that as your child grows they will want to tackle a more complex way of drawing (perhaps it's an image they have seen in a book) but as they begin to put pencil to paper they may have no idea where to start, causing frustration and annoyance.

With the help of our 'How to Draw' book series, this frustration will disappear as we guide your child step by step, line by line, to create their very own masterpiece!

Each illustration is deconstructed and simplified into lines and shapes which will not overwhelm your child. As we guide them to form each simple line and shape together on the paper, the image gradually becomes more detailed, textured and visually appealing. Practice will always make perfect, so encouraging your child to repeat the initial steps will incite a sense of self assurance that they are able to improve their skill line by line.

If Your Child Struggles With This Book

The rate of cognitive development varies from child to child and, as such, where one child may be ready for this book another will not. If you feel that your child is not ready for this book at the moment, take it away and bring it back to them in six to twelve months.

If your child is not ready to draw step-by-step, he or she may prefer to work using grids. Grid drawing involves copying information from one grid to another using coordinates. The type of copying required in grid drawing is very useful for the brain as, in particular, it exercises working memory. Working memory involves holding onto information temporarily and then using that temporarily held information at the same time. Working memory is an important process required in maintaining attention and exercising it will be beneficial for a range of activities, including in class at school.

Dr James Manning
Consultant Clinical Psychologist

For the webpage and password for your bonus books please see bottom of page 40.

HOW TO DRAW KOALAS

Here are all of the drawings in this book. I guess it must seem like there is a lot of them when they are looked at all at once!

Luckily, I am not going to ask you to draw them all straight away. The best way to learn to draw is one step at a time. Each drawing in this book may require between 50 and 200 strokes of your pencil, but all you will need to think about is drawing one stroke at a time.

As you use your pencil, stroke by stroke, working your way through this book, you will eventually be able to create all of the drawings!

Drawing Step-by-Step

In this book I will show you how to create 39 different drawings step by step. Each step will build on the previous one until eventually you have 39 complete drawings.

To make things easier for you, please download the outline grids for the drawings. You can download this additional book with all of them inside for free by visiting the web address below:

https://www.lipdf.com/product/koalas2/

At first, you find my step-by-step approach too complicated or difficult please leave it to one side and come back to it later. Instead, you may want to use an alternative grid with numbers and letters on it first. By following the coordinates and matching them up with the coordinates on a blank grid you can redraw the pictures this way instead.

I have put details below about where you can download these basic grids for free on the internet.

https://www.lipdf.com/product/grids/

You can of course ask an adult to help you draw the grids instead, or you may even feel able to draw them yourself.

Please see page 40 for the webpage address for your bonus books and the password.

1. It's okay to feel a little daunted about trying to draw this character, but always remember to take it one step at a time.

Suggested outline sketch

How to draw using a grid. You can download blank grids to practice with in dark and light PDF formats by following the link below.

https://www.lipdf.com/product/grids/

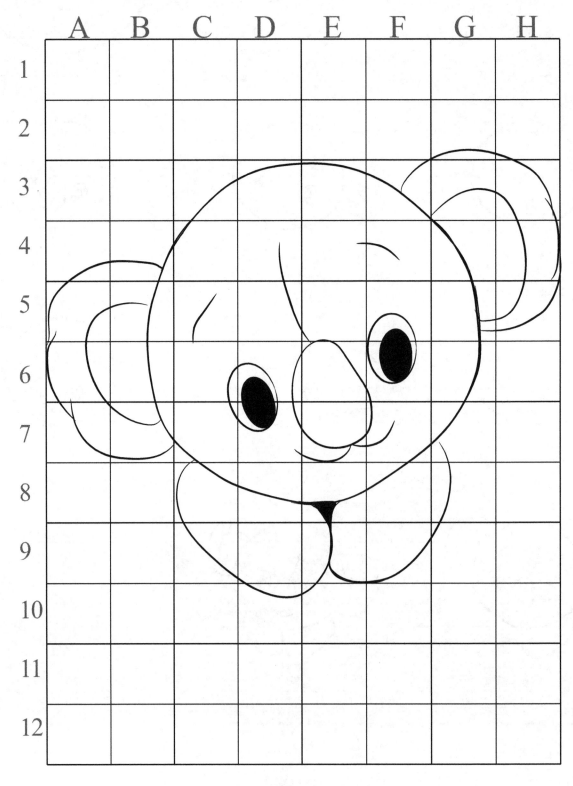

2. As you gain confidence whilst learning to draw, try brainstorming ideas for your next project! Take inspiration from all the characters in this book, and create your very own character.

Suggested outline sketch

How to draw using a grid. You can download blank grids to practice with in dark and light PDF formats by following the link below.

https://www.lipdf.com/product/grids/

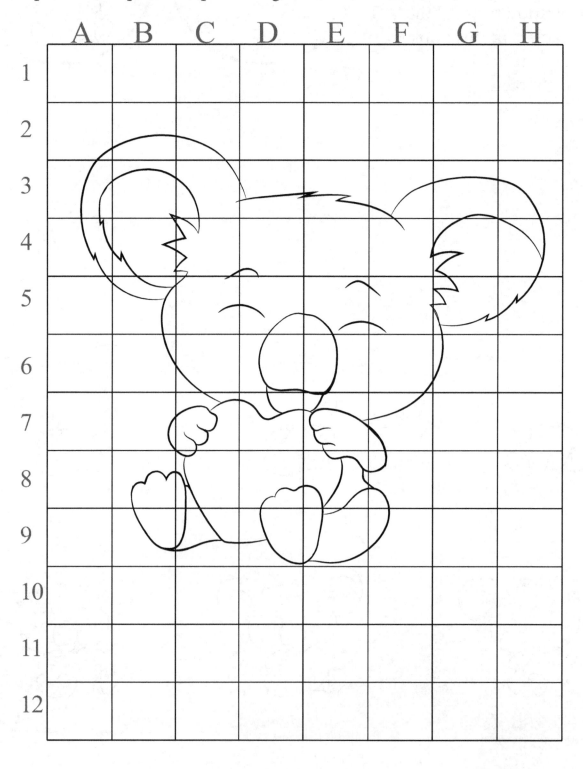

3. Try making the arms or legs longer. You'll be surprised how it dramatically alters the look of the character.

Suggested outline sketch

How to draw using a grid. You can download blank grids to practice with in dark and light PDF formats by following the link below.

https://www.lipdf.com/product/grids/

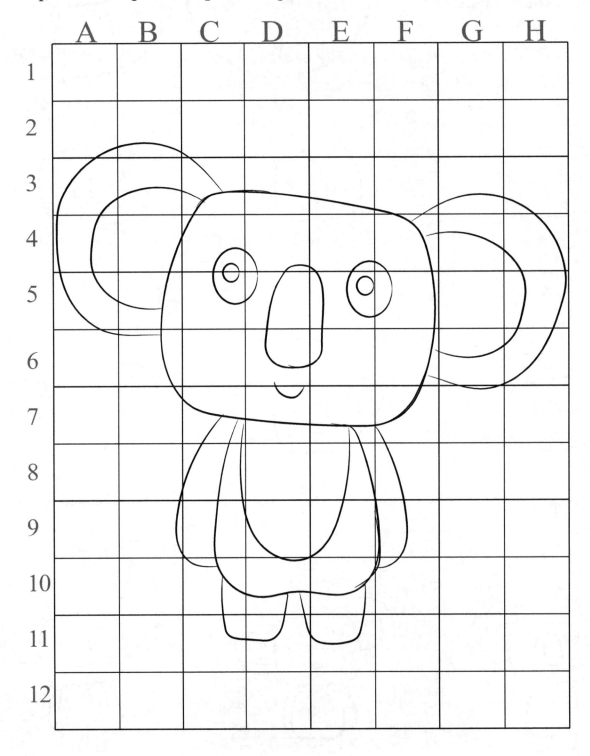

4. You can create interesting looks by changing features in your drawing.

Suggested outline sketch

How to draw using a grid. You can download blank grids to practice with in dark and light PDF formats by following the link below.

https://www.lipdf.com/product/grids/

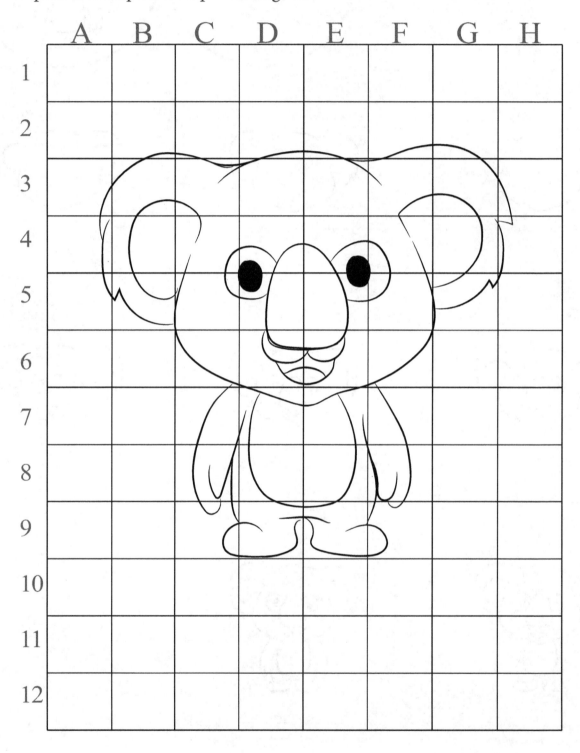

5. Try mixing different parts of drawings from this book to see what you can come up with.

Suggested outline sketch

How to draw using a grid. You can download blank grids to practice with in dark and light PDF formats by following the link below.

https://www.lipdf.com/product/grids/

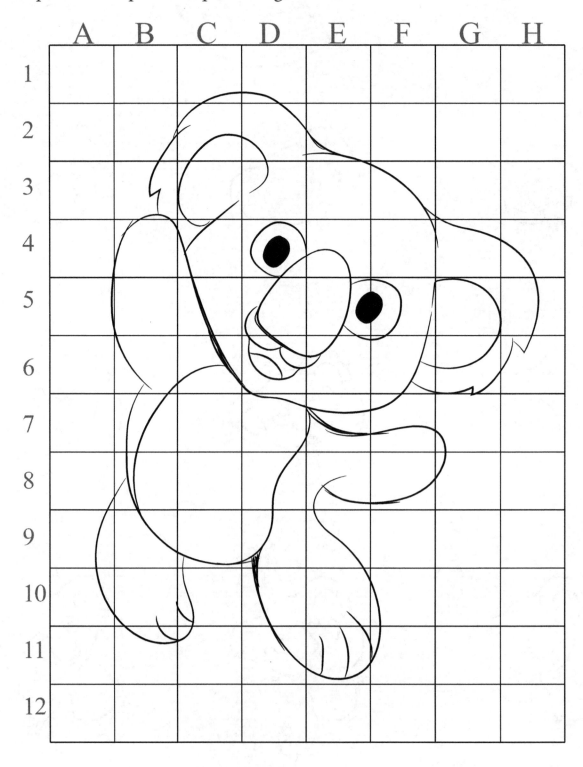

6. Sketch out your drawings one step at a time as shown below. After you have repeated this process a few times draw your own variations.

Suggested outline sketch

How to draw using a grid. You can download blank grids to practice with in dark and light PDF formats by following the link below.

https://www.lipdf.com/product/grids/

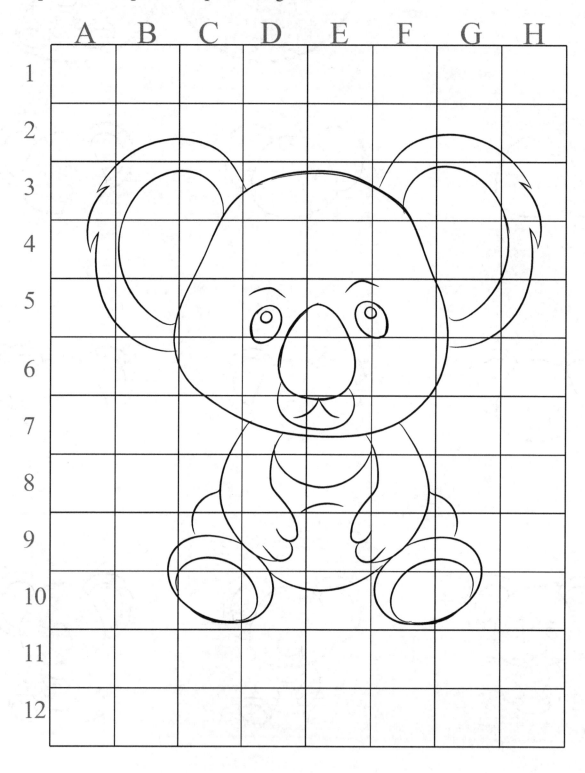

7. An ellipse is a circle that is not regular in shape. Ellipses can be very useful to add in your outline sketches when you are looking to draw circular shapes.

Suggested outline sketch

How to draw using a grid. You can download blank grids to practice with in dark and light PDF formats by following the link below.

https://www.lipdf.com/product/grids/

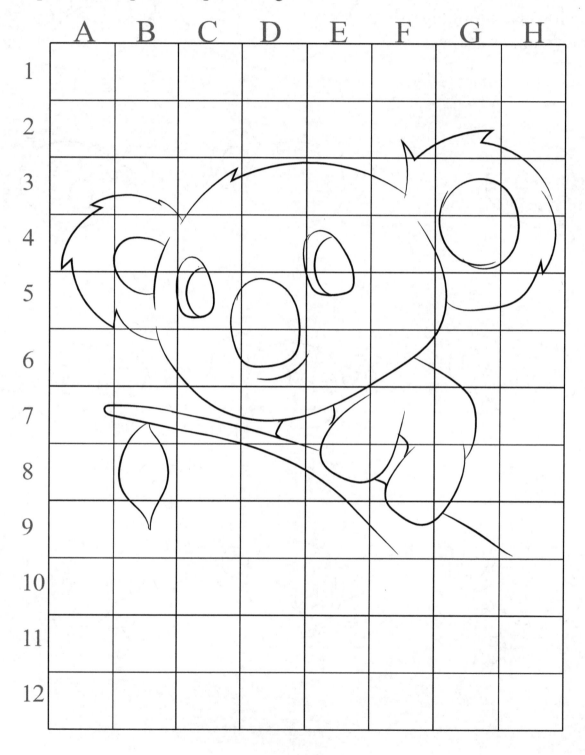

8. When you are sketching an outline, use a pencil and place as little pressure as possible on your pencil to make the lines very feint. This will make it easier to rub out later.

Suggested outline sketch

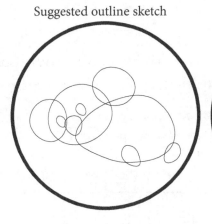

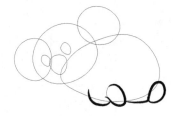

How to draw using a grid. You can download blank grids to practice with in dark and light PDF formats by following the link below.

https://www.lipdf.com/product/grids/

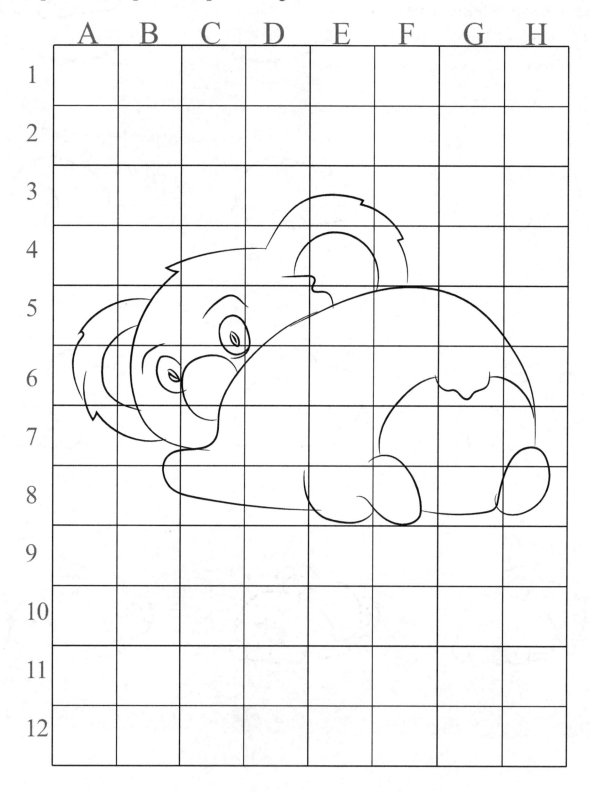

9. There are often simple steps involved in drawing that you can repeat over and over again.

How to draw using a grid. You can download blank grids to practice with in dark and light PDF formats by following the link below.

https://www.lipdf.com/product/grids/

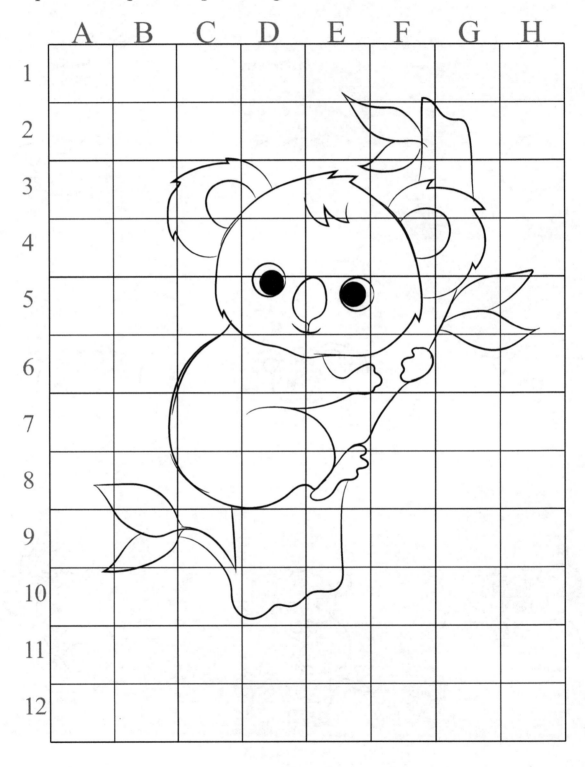

10. The first thing to do is to sketch an outline of what you would like to draw.

How to draw using a grid. You can download blank grids to practice with in dark and light PDF formats by following the link below.

https://www.lipdf.com/product/grids/

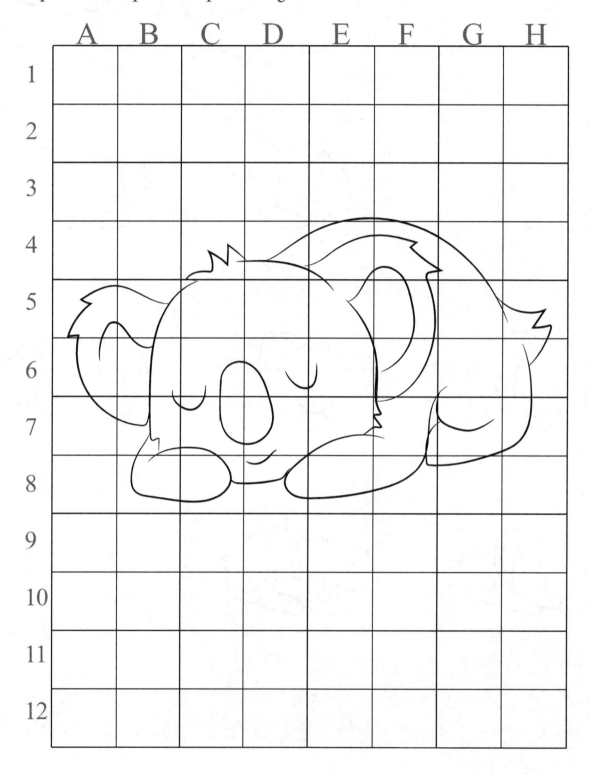

11. You can develop the direction your drawing takes with the use of a few carefully positioned lines on your initial sketch.

Suggested outline sketch

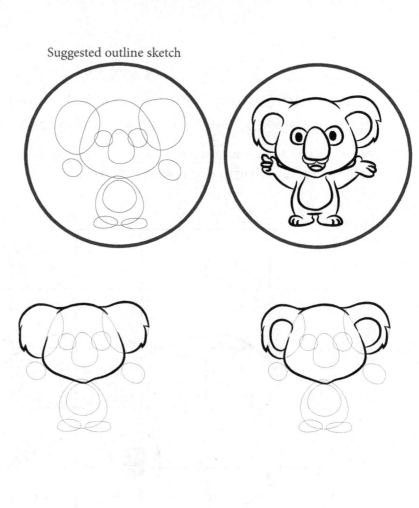

How to draw using a grid. You can download blank grids to practice with in dark and light PDF formats by following the link below.

https://www.lipdf.com/product/grids/

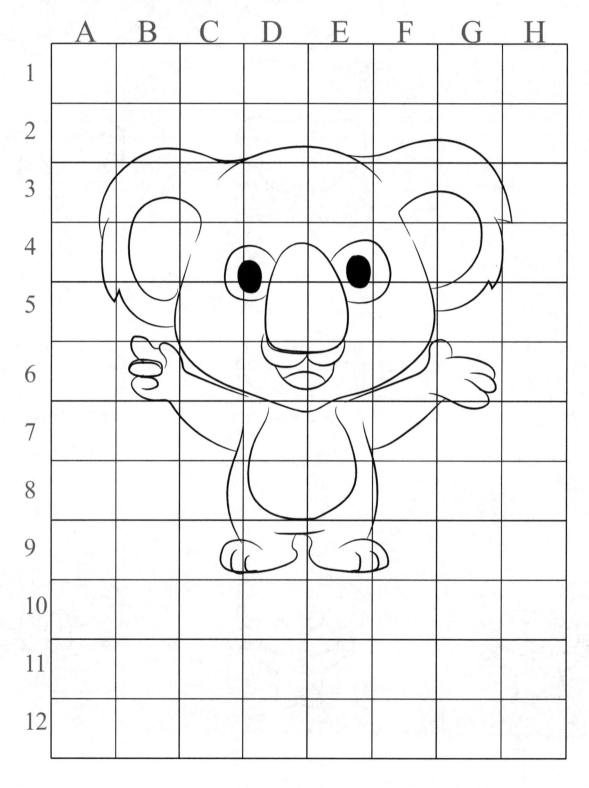

12. Remember to take regular breaks, this will help boost your concentration and prevent you from getting too tired.

Suggested outline sketch

How to draw using a grid. You can download blank grids to practice with in dark and light PDF formats by following the link below.

https://www.lipdf.com/product/grids/

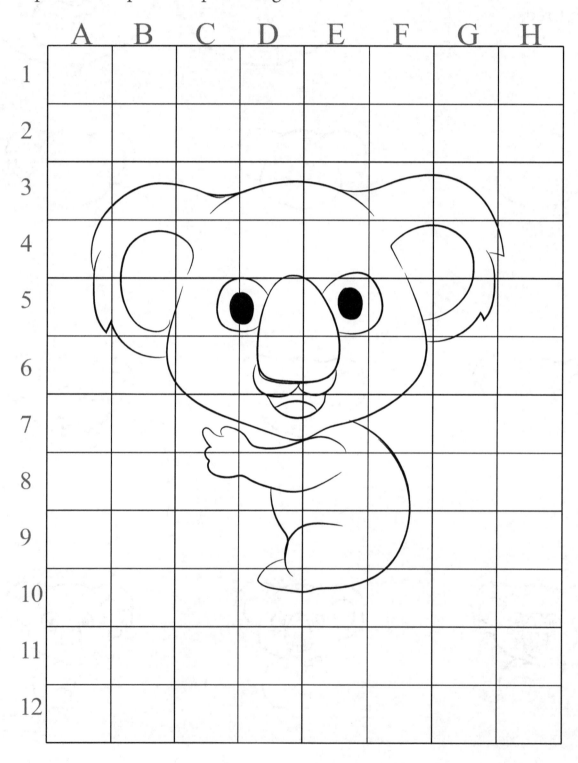

13. The extra line or shape you may have drawn accidently, could become part of the drawing as a whole and copying the lines exactly as they are in this drawing isn't a necessity.

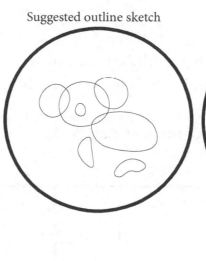

How to draw using a grid. You can download blank grids to practice with in dark and light PDF formats by following the link below.

https://www.lipdf.com/product/grids/

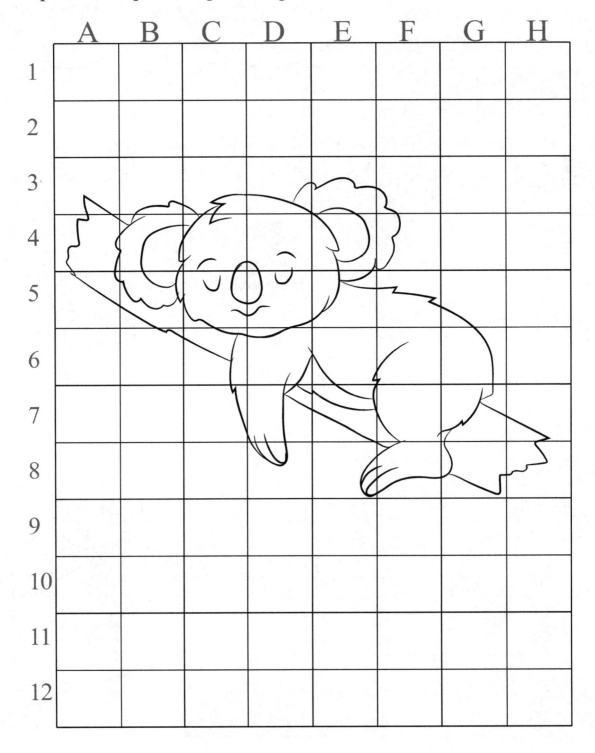

14. Think about your drawing as lots of small parts. Focus on drawing one part at a time and then go onto the next part. All the parts will add up at the end!

Suggested outline sketch

How to draw using a grid. You can download blank grids to practice with in dark and light PDF formats by following the link below.

https://www.lipdf.com/product/grids/

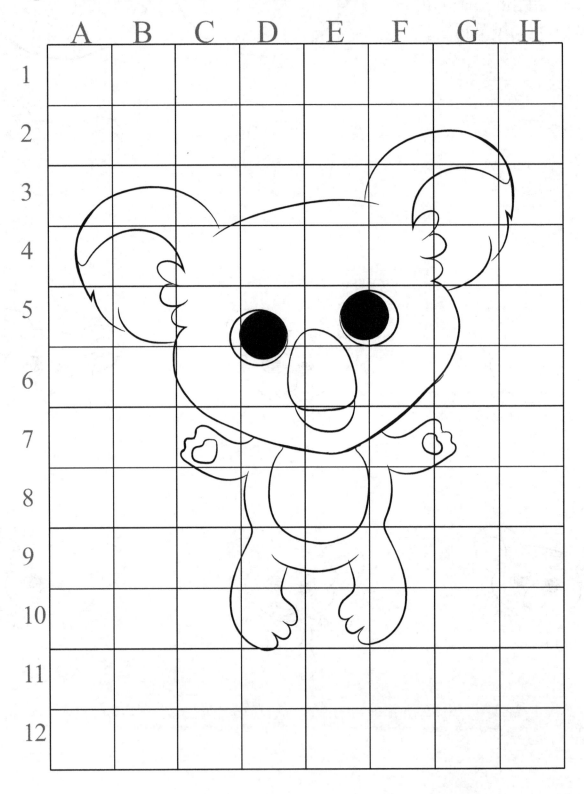

15. Begin by deciding where you want the character's head, torso, legs and arms to be positioned.

Suggested outline sketch

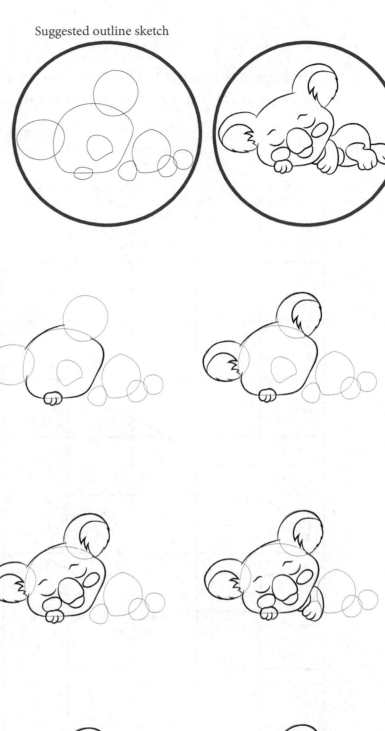

How to draw using a grid. You can download blank grids to practice with in dark and light PDF formats by following the link below.

https://www.lipdf.com/product/grids/

16. Drawing stimulates parts of the brain that are responsible for creative thinking and imagination. From a young age, we are all creatively encouraged to draw, often to improve our fine motor skills and co-ordination.

Suggested outline sketch

How to draw using a grid. You can download blank grids to practice with in dark and light PDF formats by following the link below.

https://www.lipdf.com/product/grids/

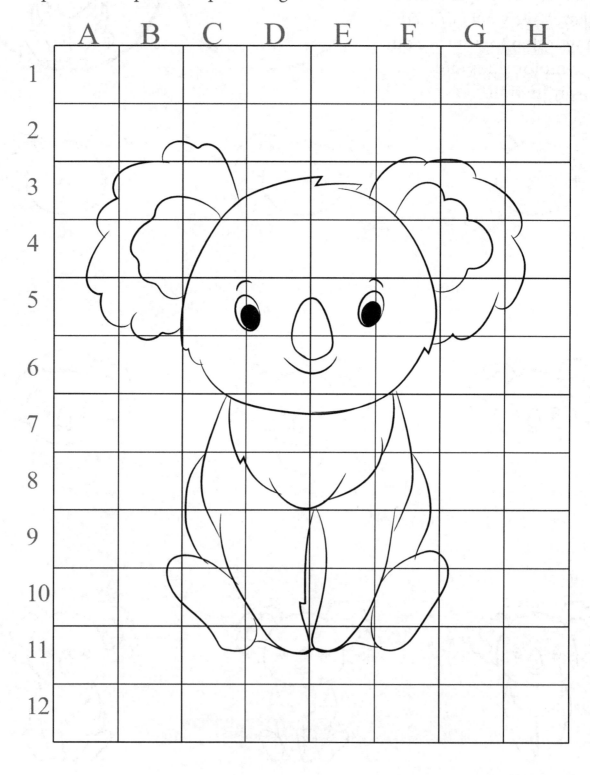

17. Drawing a basic outline will help you to give your picture good proportions. Sketch this out as lightly as possible so that it is just barely visible.

Alternatively, print out the outline sketch first using this book's templates.

Suggested outline sketch

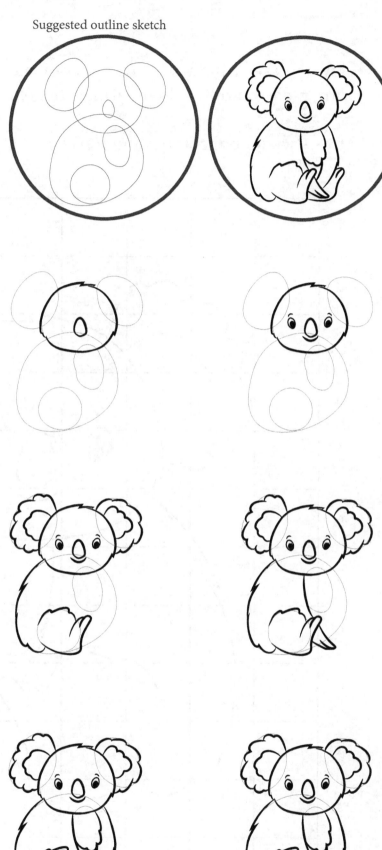

How to draw using a grid. You can download blank grids to practice with in dark and light PDF formats by following the link below.

https://www.lipdf.com/product/grids/

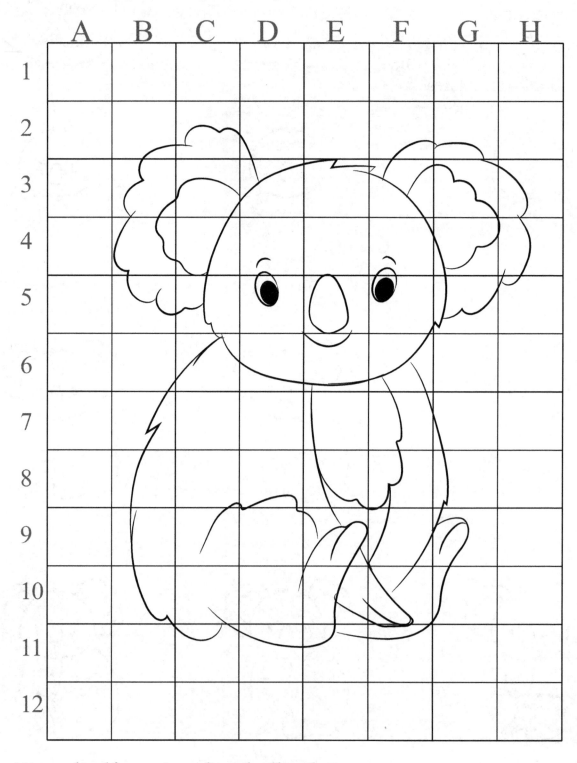

18. Begin by deciding where you want the character's head and major joints to be positioned. Follow this up with the character's limbs.

Suggested outline sketch

How to draw using a grid. You can download blank grids to practice with in dark and light PDF formats by following the link below.

https://www.lipdf.com/product/grids/

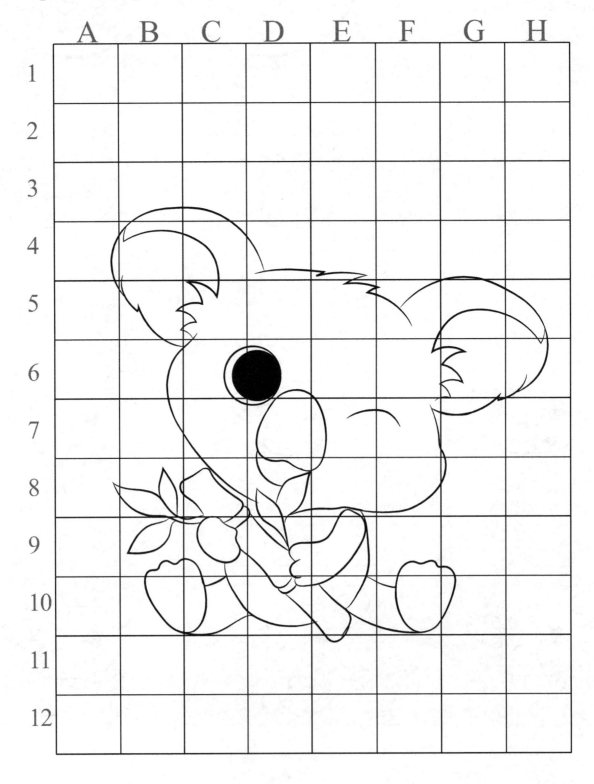

19. If a project looks too difficult to complete all in one go, complete part of it and come back to it a little later. It will then feel less overwhelming.

Suggested outline sketch

How to draw using a grid. You can download blank grids to practice with in dark and light PDF formats by following the link below.

https://www.lipdf.com/product/grids/

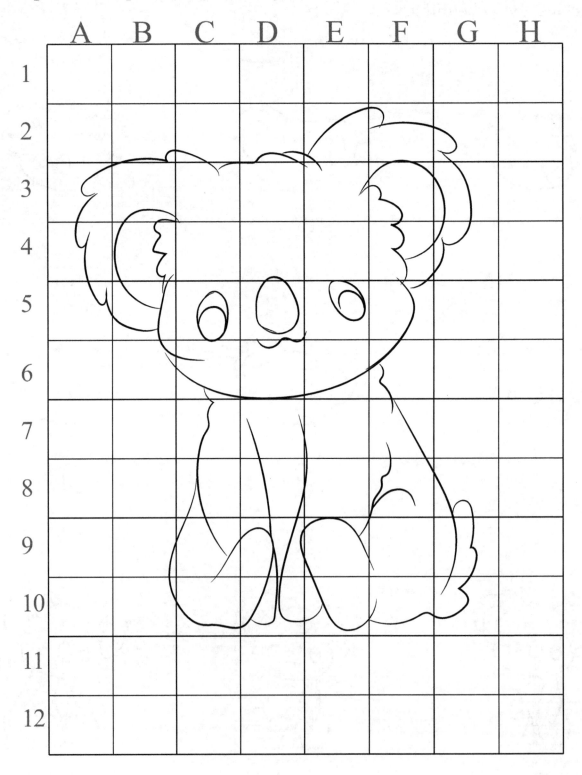

20. If you find that you are rushing, stop what you are doing and take a break. Rushing too much will reduce the quality of your work.

Suggested outline sketch

How to draw using a grid. You can download blank grids to practice with in dark and light PDF formats by following the link below.

https://www.lipdf.com/product/grids/

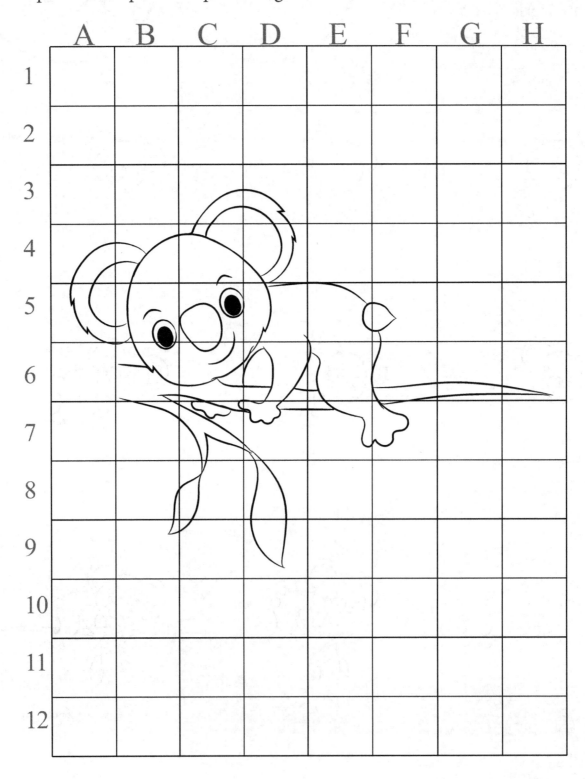

21. If you are struggling for ideas for your work, take a break and do something different. Your mind will keep working in the background for you. Some of our greatest ideas come to us while we sleep.

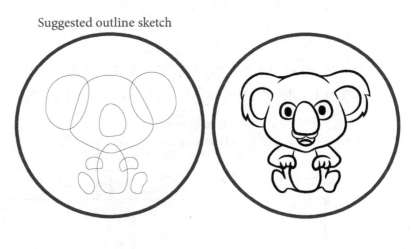

How to draw using a grid. You can download blank grids to practice with in dark and light PDF formats by following the link below.

https://www.lipdf.com/product/grids/

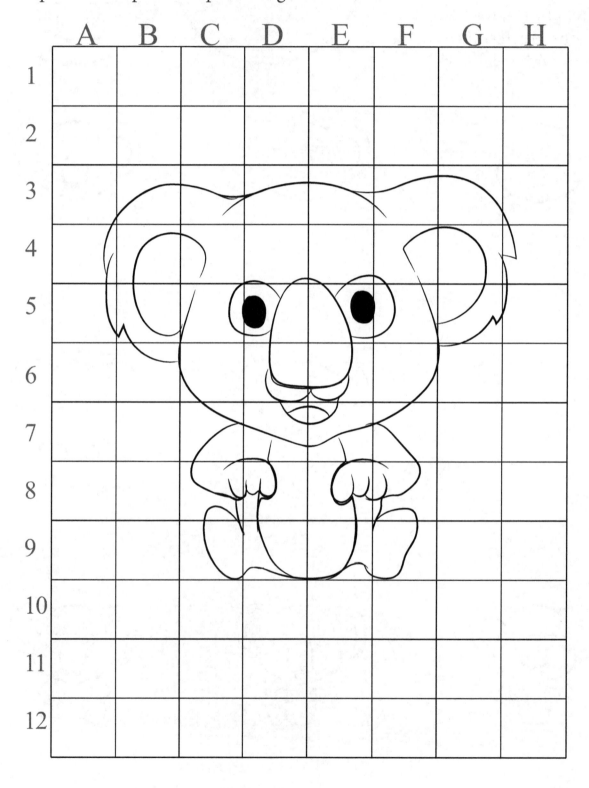

22. For larger projects focus on one step at a time. People have walked thousands of miles by taking one step at a time.

Suggested outline sketch

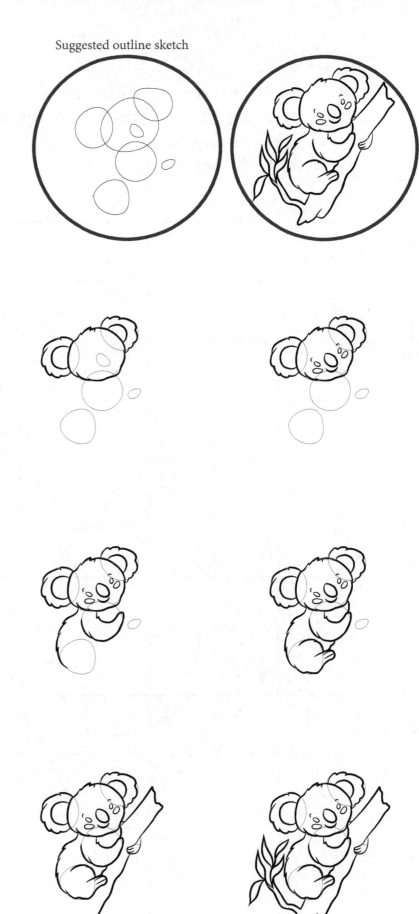

How to draw using a grid. You can download blank grids to practice with in dark and light PDF formats by following the link below.

https://www.lipdf.com/product/grids/

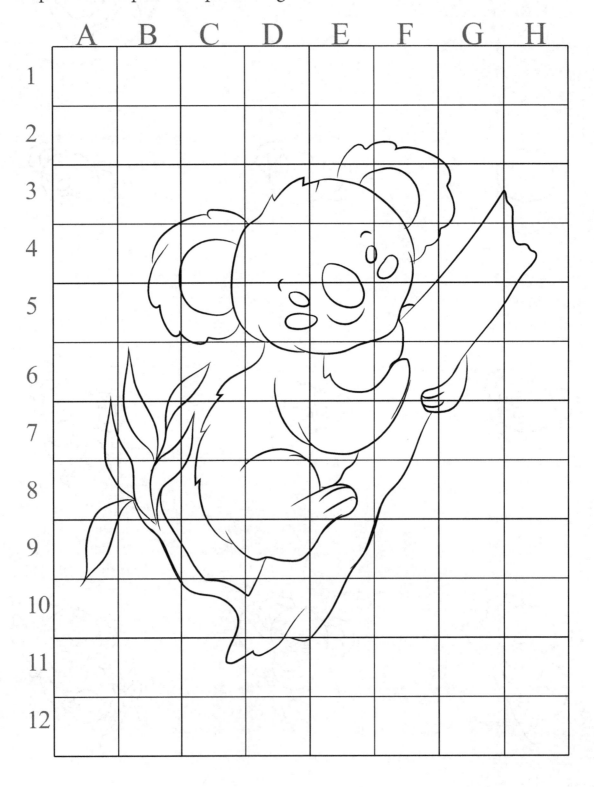

23. Taking photographs from different angles and then tracing them can often help with laying out the proportions of a figure or an object.

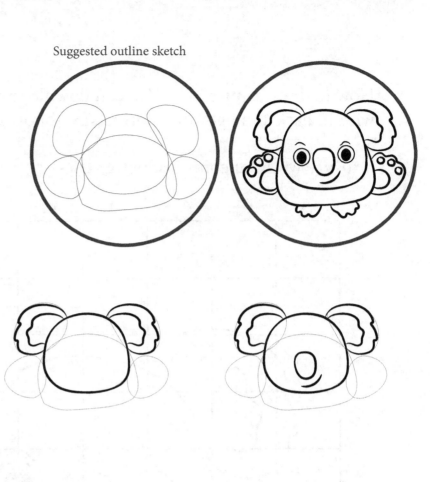

How to draw using a grid. You can download blank grids to practice with in dark and light PDF formats by following the link below.

https://www.lipdf.com/product/grids/

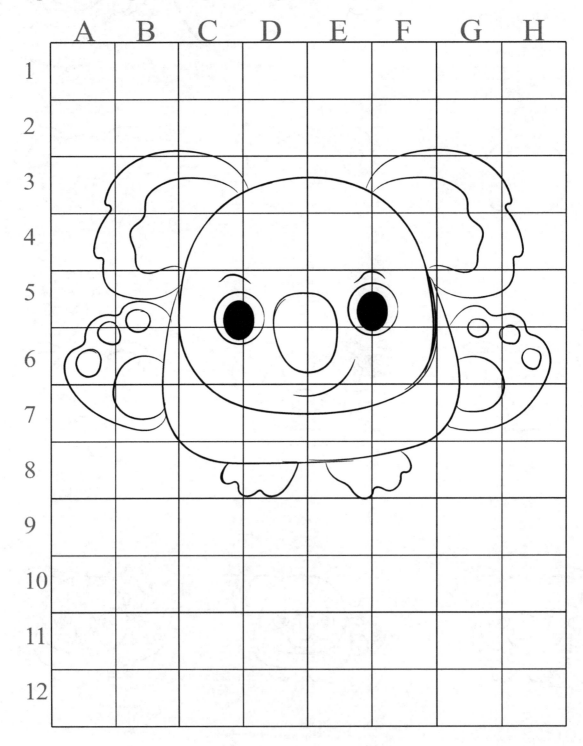

24. We all make mistakes, even the most successful people in life do. What sets successful people apart is how they respond to their mistakes.

How to draw using a grid. You can download blank grids to practice with in dark and light PDF formats by following the link below.

https://www.lipdf.com/product/grids/

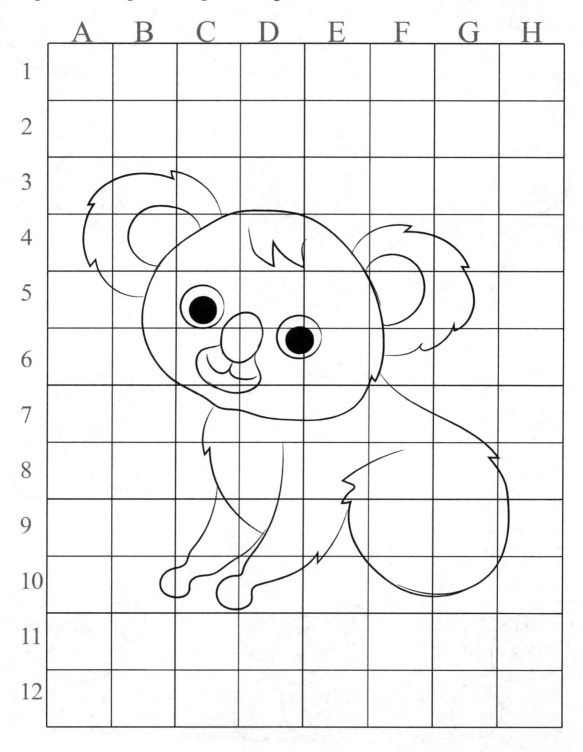

25. To become an expert at something you may need to spend thousands of hours doing it. Expert artists will often have spent more than 10,000 hours practising. Every minute you spend drawing will add up.

How to draw using a grid. You can download blank grids to practice with in dark and light PDF formats by following the link below.

https://www.lipdf.com/product/grids/

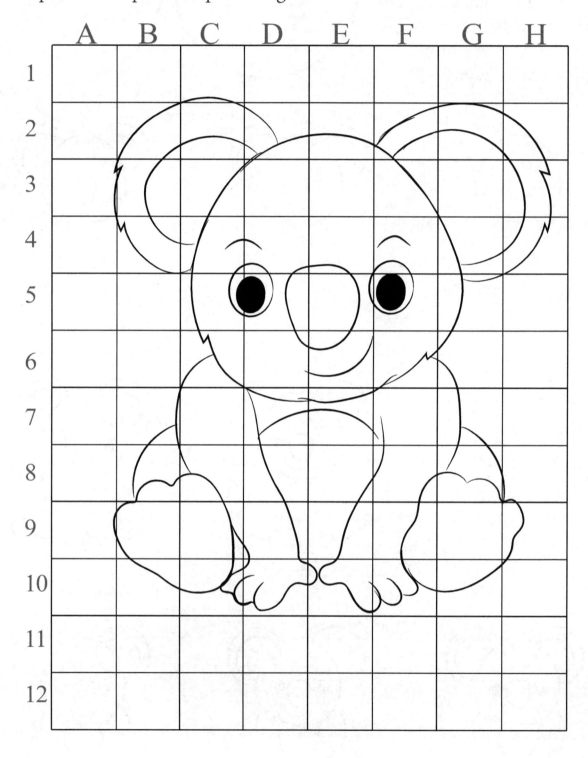

26. Try swapping part of
your drawing with the
part of another from this
book. This can lead to
very interesting creations.

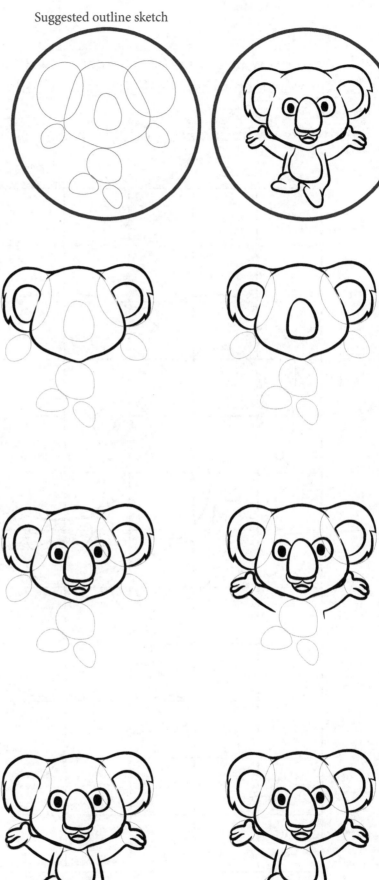

How to draw using a grid. You can download blank grids to practice with in dark and light PDF formats by following the link below.

https://www.lipdf.com/product/grids/

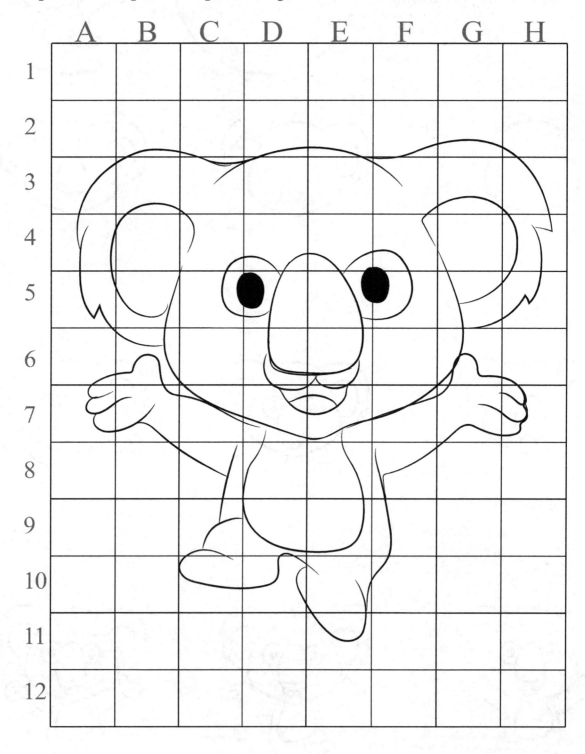

27. It can be very difficult to get things right the first time, but remember the more you draw the better you will get at it.

Suggested outline sketch

How to draw using a grid. You can download blank grids to practice with in dark and light PDF formats by following the link below.

https://www.lipdf.com/product/grids/

28. It is very rare to see animals of the same breed that are exactly alike. It is usually small details that separate them.

Suggested outline sketch

61

How to draw using a grid. You can download blank grids to practice with in dark and light PDF formats by following the link below.

https://www.lipdf.com/product/grids/

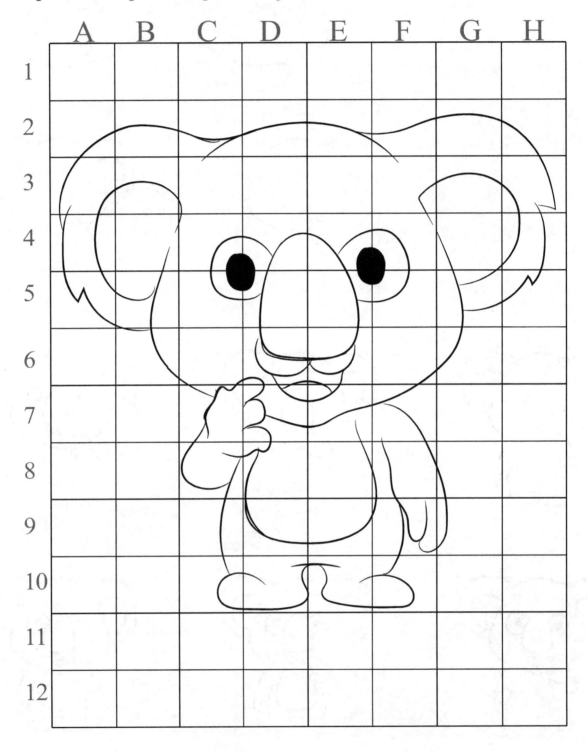

29. The more information you can fit on your initial outline sketch, the easier it will be to structure your drawing.

Suggested outline sketch

How to draw using a grid. You can download blank grids to practice with in dark and light PDF formats by following the link below.

https://www.lipdf.com/product/grids/

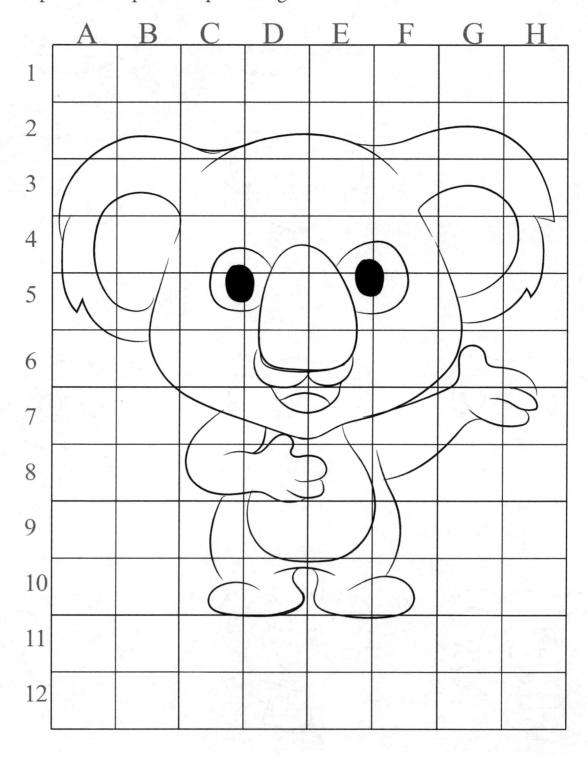

30. You can build your drawing around a rough outline sketch and making it up as you go along.

Suggested outline sketch

How to draw using a grid. You can download blank grids to practice with in dark and light PDF formats by following the link below.

https://www.lipdf.com/product/grids/

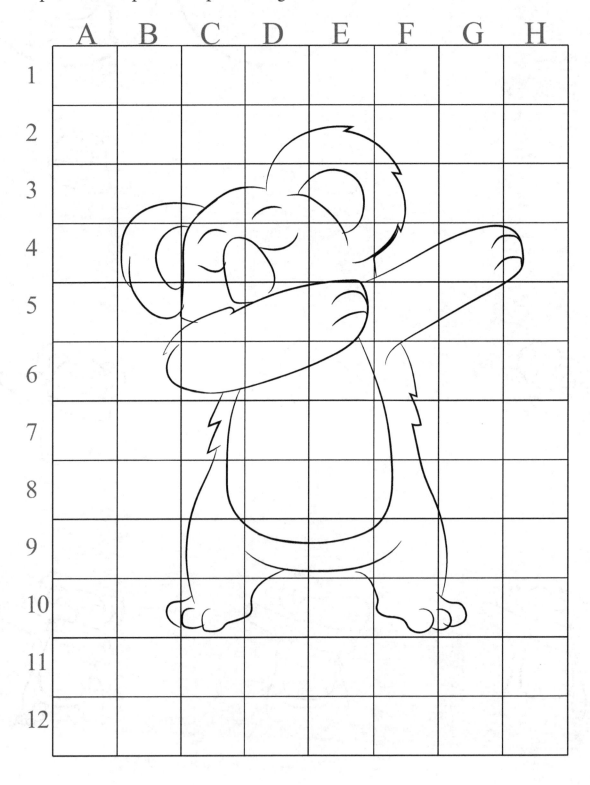

31. Your drawing may have a basic shape that you can attempt to sketch out before you start drawing.

Suggested outline sketch

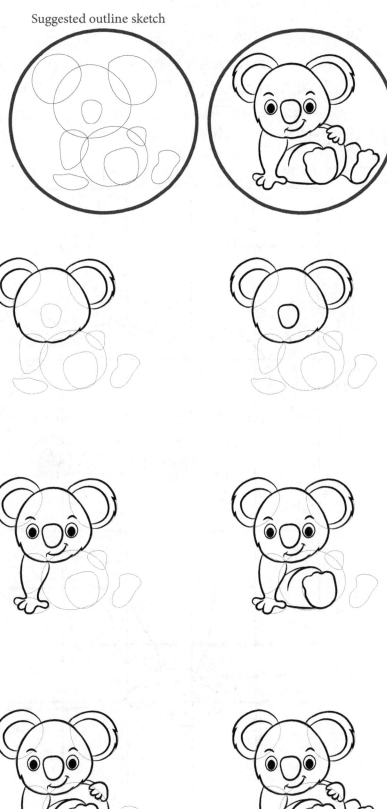

How to draw using a grid. You can download blank grids to practice with in dark and light PDF formats by following the link below.

https://www.lipdf.com/product/grids/

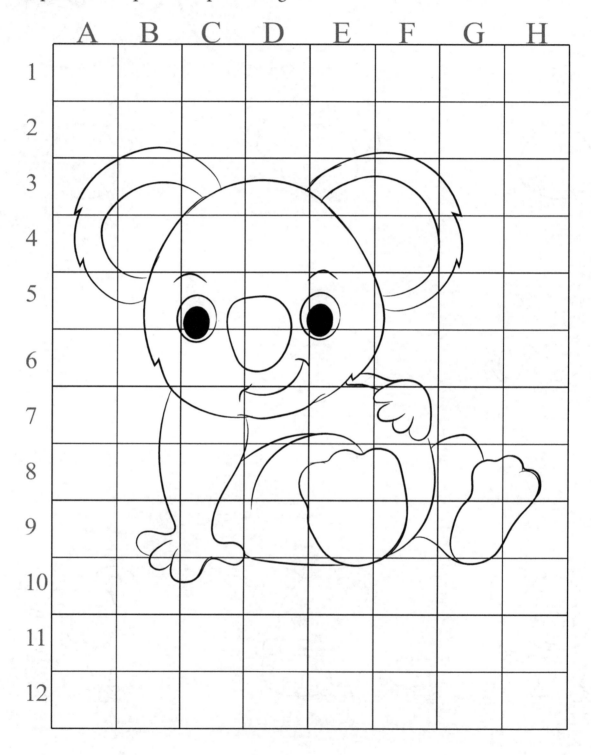

32. Try altering your drawing slightly to create a different look.

Suggested outline sketch

How to draw using a grid. You can download blank grids to practice with in dark and light PDF formats by following the link below.

https://www.lipdf.com/product/grids/

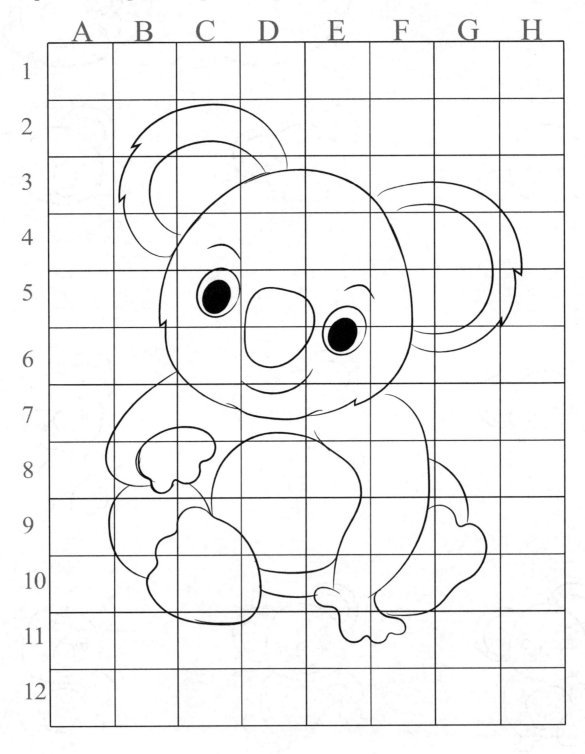

33. Once you become more proficient you can draw your own outline sketches and following that refine them.

Suggested outline sketch

How to draw using a grid. You can download blank grids to practice with in dark and light PDF formats by following the link below.

https://www.lipdf.com/product/grids/

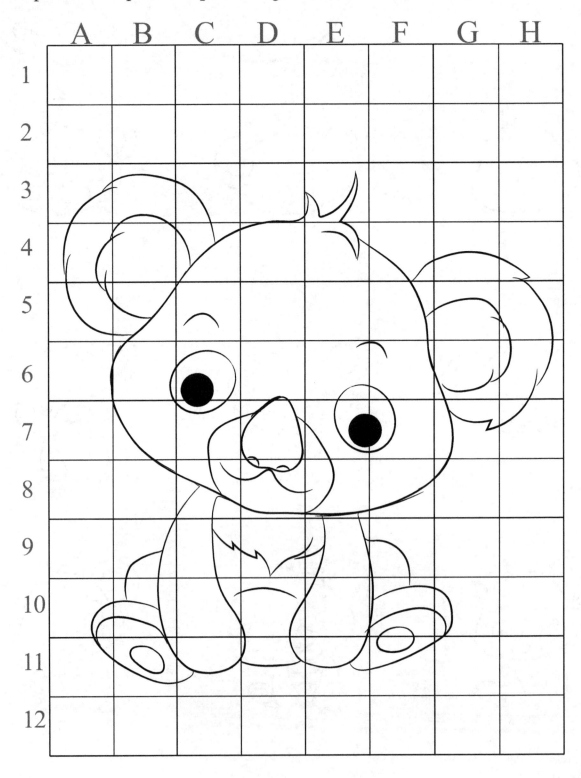

34. Ask questions to stimulate your creativity. Following this, listen to the suggestions your mind comes up with.

Suggested outline sketch

How to draw using a grid. You can download blank grids to practice with in dark and light PDF formats by following the link below.

https://www.lipdf.com/product/grids/

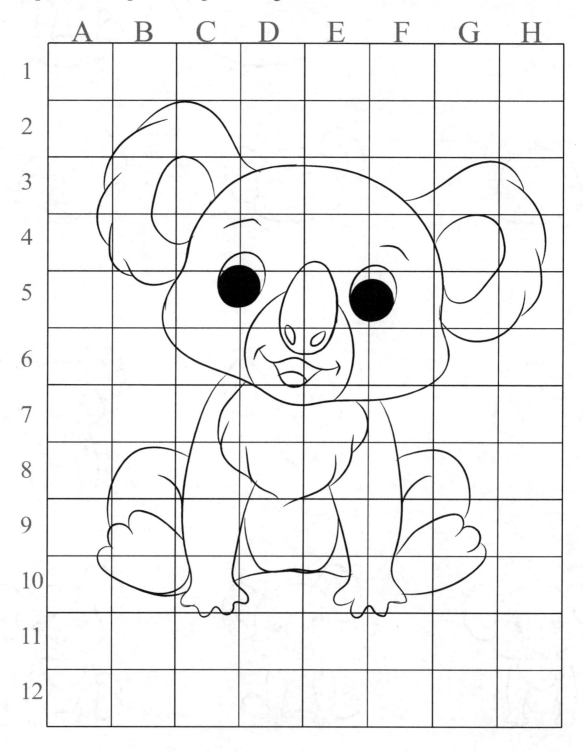

35. After you have sketched out this drawing step by step, add extra features to make it look more original or personal to you.

Suggested outline sketch

How to draw using a grid. You can download blank grids to practice with in dark and light PDF formats by following the link below.

https://www.lipdf.com/product/grids/

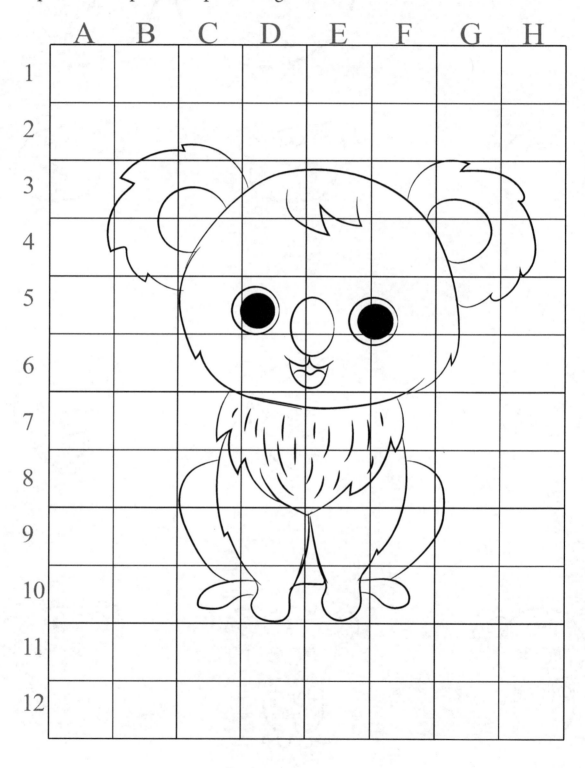

36. Separate your initial sketch into sections to help you decide how you want to proportion your drawing. This can help you to alter the height of your character.

Suggested outline sketch

How to draw using a grid. You can download blank grids to practice with in dark and light PDF formats by following the link below.

https://www.lipdf.com/product/grids/

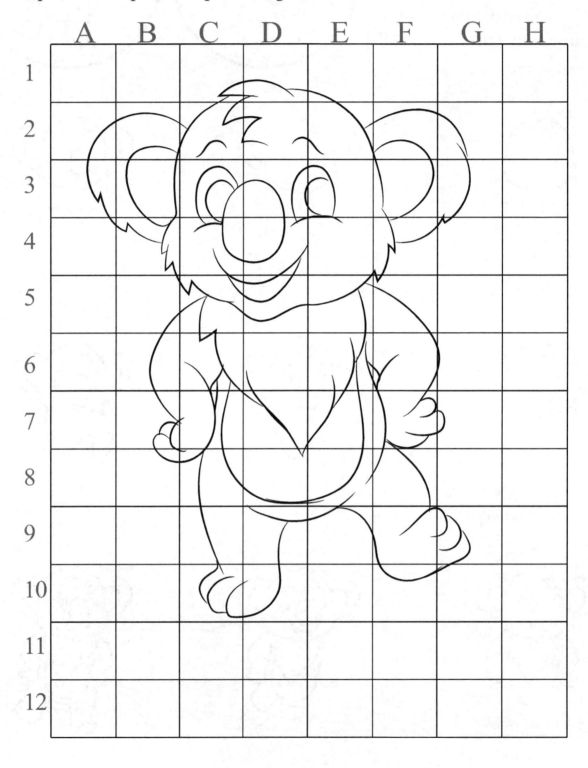

37. To give your brain a workout, complete a drawing in an opposite way to way you would normally approach it. Sometimes this can help us see things that we did not notice before.

Suggested outline sketch

How to draw using a grid. You can download blank grids to practice with in dark and light PDF formats by following the link below.

https://www.lipdf.com/product/grids/

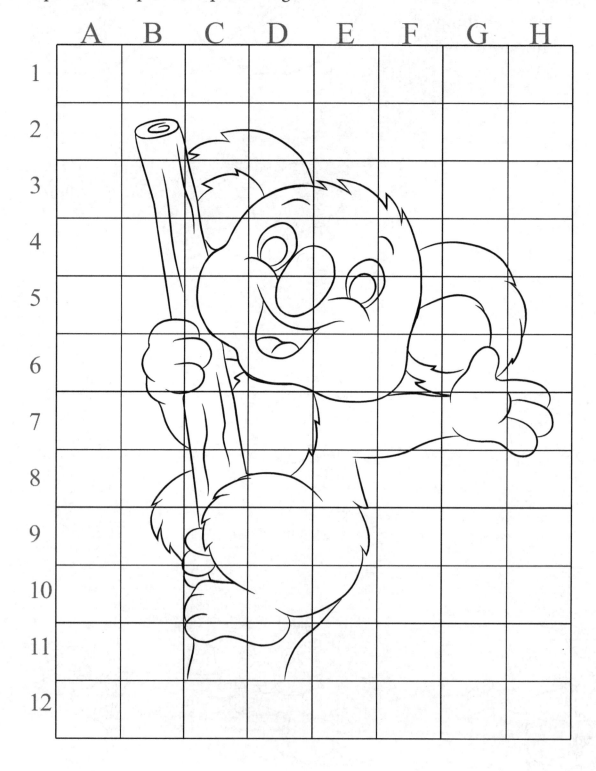

38. You can develop the direction the head of your drawing takes with the use of a few carefully positioned lines on your initial sketch.

Suggested outline sketch

How to draw using a grid. You can download blank grids to practice with in dark and light PDF formats by following the link below.

https://www.lipdf.com/product/grids/

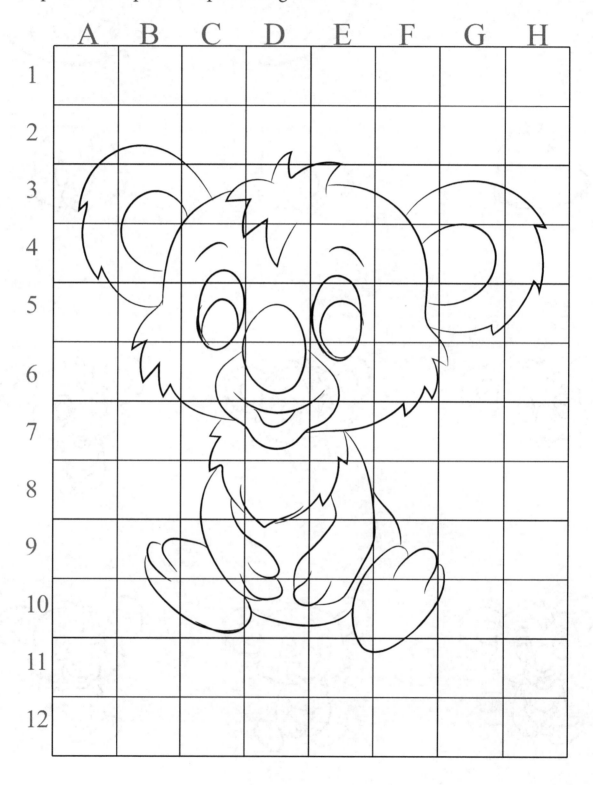

39. Just as the body needs exercise to remain fit and healthy, so does the brain. The more exercise you give you brain the more effective it becomes.

Suggested outline sketch

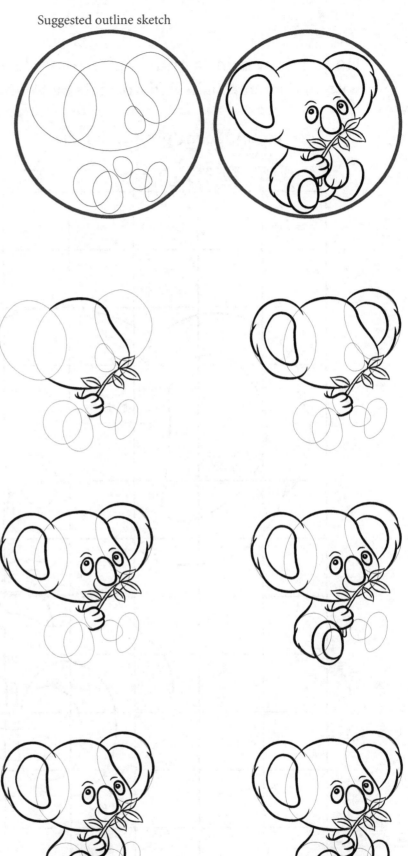

How to draw using a grid. You can download blank grids to practice with in dark and light PDF formats by following the link below.

https://www.lipdf.com/product/grids/

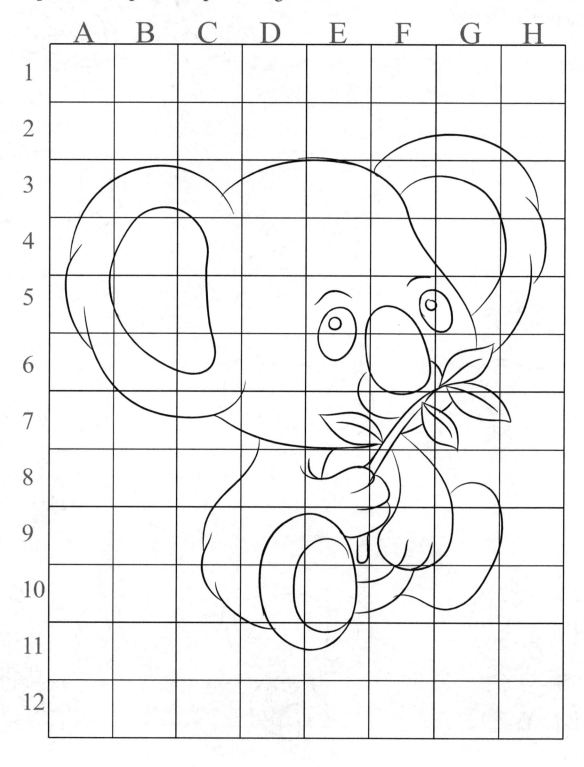

CPSIA information can be obtained
at www.ICGtesting.com
Printed in the USA
LVHW060713270321
682665LV00022B/282